WE ARE

PENN STATE !

Thank you for supporting me by purchasing this book.
I hope you enjoy it as much as I did in helping make it.
I am looking forward to seeing and hearing you at the stadium!

LANDON TENGWALL 58

ISBN: 979-8-218-07274-2
Published by Exit 56 Publications, LLC. Marietta, GA 30062

Our contact information: Exit56Publications@gmail.com
Or visit our website: www.shopexit56.com

MAXPREPS AND USA
TODAY ALL AMERICAN

RATED NO. 8 OFFENSIVE
TACKLE RIVALS

FOUR YEAR HIGH
SCHOOL LETTERMAN

ADIDAS ALL AMERICAN BOWL
UNDER ARMOUR ALL AMERICAN
BOWL AND POLYNESIAN BOWL

While Landon always enjoyed playing football, he excelled in a unique sport when he was younger. Water polo! He played for the US Naval Academy Juniors team.

How good was young Landon at water polo? Good enough to be a Junior Olympian and win several Gold Medals!

But it was football that was always his true love. Long before Landon made the trip from Olney, MD to Happy Valley, he and his friends played football on the sandlots dreaming that one day he would be playing big time football.

2010
Vs Northwestern 35-21
McGloin takes the snap. He's looking
for Moye on the sidelines. He's got it!
Touchdown, Penn State!

1982
Vs Nebraska 27-24
Blackledge is leading the team down the field. Nine seconds on the clock. He's looking for McCloskey down the sideline. He's got it! Touchdown, Penn State!

2006

Florida State 26-23 (Orange Bowl)
Penn State and Florida St have swapped a couple of missed field goals. The Nittany Lions will once more put their faith in freshman kicker Kelly. From 29 yards out...it's good! Winner, Penn State!

THEN HIS
INTO

DREAMS TURNED
REALITY

Fight on State (GO!)
Fight on State (GO!)

When I'm on the field I am always pumped up and ready to go. The adrenaline is flowing and then I hear this from the best fans in world and I know that Victory will be ours.

Start Me Up

If you start me up
If you start me up, I'll never stop
If you start me up
If you start me up, I'll never stop

Ten Questions with Landon Tengwall

1. What is your favorite dinner time meal?
A big ribeye with mashed potatoes and broccoli.
I would also get a Shirley Temple as my drink.

2. Where are you taking someone on a first date?
On a picnic in a beautiful park or on a lake somewhere.
I would bring sandwiches, fruit, and BBQ chips.

3. Favorite music group or genre:
Rap and Hip Hop are my favorite genres, but
I also like country music as well as R&B.

4. Place you want to visit that you haven't been to:
Bora Bora, Arizona and Greece. Bora Bora is where
I want to go on vacation once I make it to the NFL.

5. Pets:
I don't have any pets.

6. Person you'd like to have dinner with from the past:
Muhammad Ali. I'd love to hear his stories about his journey from boxing to being a huge civil rights activist.

7. Person you'd like to have dinner with from present:
Larry Allen. I would pick his brain all night about OL technique and what is was like playing for the Cowboys in the 90s.

8. Favorite vacation spot
Outer Banks, NC. My family and I have been going every Thanksgiving since I was born. We rent a big beach house and stay for a week.

9. Places you have lived:
Annapolis, Maryland and State College, Pennsylvania.

10. Why Penn State?
The coaches and brotherhood are what has meant the most to me. The coaches love you like sons and are always there for you. I have a blast with all my teammates creating lifelong memories and friends.

When Landon is not playing football he enjoys playing video games, cooking and collecting shoes. His favorite video games are Madden, NBA 2K and Call of Duty.

One of Landon's special talents is cooking. He has his own special recipe to marinate steak: one part honey and two parts soy sauce. Then he makes mashed potatoes and roasted broccoli as sides. Mmmm!

One of Landon's favorite hobbies is collecting shoes. His favorites are Nike's Air Jordan 1 Travis Scotts, Size 15.

BUT THEN IT'S
BACK TO WORK

Landon lifts weights 7 days a week all year around. He's bench pressed 225lbs 31 times, already at the NFL combine average. When he goes heavy he benches 445 lbs.

He squats 540 pounds doing 5 reps per set. That weight added up is the equivalent of putting a pick up truck on his shoulders.

Landon power cleans 325lbs and has his sights on Barkely's Penn State weight room record!

NO BETTER WAY
TO END A GAME

And Penn St wins it!

How Well Do You Know

Landon's favorite shoes are?
a) Nike
b) Adidas
c) Converse

One of Landon's favorite snacks is:
a) Apples
b) Pretzels
c) BBQ Chips

Landon generally lifts weights:
a) 3 times a week
b) 5 times a week
c) 7 times a week

LANDON TENGWALL ?

What Other sport does Landon excel at?
a) Water Polo
b) Baseball
c) Tennis

Landon favorite vacation is:
a) Going to the city
b) Going to the the beach
c) Going to the mountains

One of Landon's dream vacations is to visit:
a) Italy
b) France
c) Greece